Your Government:
How It Works

The Attorney General's Office

Daniel E. Harmon

Arthur M. Schlesinger, jr.
Senior Consulting Editor

Chelsea House Publishers
Philadelphia

CHELSEA HOUSE PUBLISHERS
Production Manager Pamela Loos
Art Director Sara Davis
Director of Photography Judy L. Hasday
Managing Editor James D. Gallagher
Senior Production Editor J. Christopher Higgins

Staff for THE ATTORNEY GENERAL'S OFFICE
Project Editor/Publishing Coordinator Jim McAvoy
Associate Art Director Takeshi Takahashi
Series Designers Takeshi Takahashi, Keith Trego

The Chelsea House World Wide Web address is
http://www.chelseahouse.com

First Printing
1 3 5 7 9 8 6 4 2

Library of Congress Cataloging-in-Publication Data

Harmon, Daniel E.
    The Attorney General's Office / Daniel Harmon.
      p. cm.—(Your government—how it works)
    Includes bibliographical references and index.
    ISBN 0-7910-5995-2
    1. United States. Dept. of Justice. Office of the Attorney
General—Juvenile literature. 2. Attorneys general—United
States—Juvenile literature. [1. United States. Dept. of Justice.
Office of the Attorney General. 2. Attorneys general. 3. Cabinet
officers.] I. Title. II. Series.

KF5107 .H28 2000
353.4'0973—dc21   00-034593

Contents

Introduction

Government: Crises of Confidence

Arthur M. Schlesinger, jr.

FROM THE START, Americans have regarded their government with a mixture of reliance and mistrust. The men who founded the republic understood the importance of government. "If men were angels," observed the 51st Federalist Paper, "no government would be necessary." But men are not angels. Because human beings are subject to wicked as well as to noble impulses, government was deemed essential to assure freedom and order.

The American revolutionaries, however, also knew that government could become a source of injury and oppression. The men who gathered in Philadelphia in 1787 to write the Constitution therefore had two purposes in mind: They wanted to establish a strong central authority and to limit that central authority's capacity to abuse its power.

To prevent the abuse of power, the Founding Fathers wrote two basic principles into the Constitution. The principle of federalism divided power between the state governments and the central authority. The principle of the separation of powers subdivided the central authority itself into three branches—the executive, the legislative, and the judiciary—so that "each may be a check on the other."

YOUR GOVERNMENT: HOW IT WORKS examines some of the major parts of that central authority, the federal government. It explains how various officials, agencies, and departments operate and explores the political organizations that have grown up to serve the needs of government.

Introduction

The federal government as presented in the Constitution was more an idealistic construct than a practical administrative structure. It was barely functional when it came into being.

This was especially true of the executive branch. The Constitution did not describe the executive branch in any detail. After vesting executive power in the president, it assumed the existence of "executive departments" without specifying what these departments should be. Congress began defining their functions in 1789 by creating the Departments of State, Treasury, and War.

President Washington, assisted by Secretary of the Treasury Alexander Hamilton, equipped the infant republic with a working administrative structure. Congress also continued that process by creating more executive departments as they were needed.

Throughout the 19th century, the number of federal government workers increased at a consistently faster rate than did the population. Increasing concerns about the politicization of public service led to efforts—bitterly opposed by politicians—to reform it in the latter part of the century.

The 20th century saw considerable expansion of the federal establishment. More importantly, it saw growing impatience with bureaucracy in society as a whole.

The Great Depression during the 1930s confronted the nation with its greatest crisis since the Civil War. Under Franklin Roosevelt, the New Deal reshaped the federal government, assigning it a variety of new responsibilities and greatly expanding its regulatory functions. By 1940, the number of federal workers passed the 1 million mark.

Critics complained of big government and bureaucracy. Business owners resented federal regulation. Conservatives worried about the impact of paternalistic government on self-reliance, on community responsibility, and on economic and personal freedom.

When the United States entered World War II in 1941, government agencies focused their energies on supporting the war effort. By the end of World War II, federal civilian employment had risen to 3.8 million. With peace, the federal establishment declined to around 2 million in 1950. Then growth resumed, reaching 2.8 million by the 1980s.

A large part of this growth was the result of the national government assuming new functions such as: affirmative action in civil rights, environmental protection, and safety and health in the workplace.

Some critics became convinced that the national government was a steadily growing behemoth swallowing up the liberties of the people. The 1980s brought new intensity to the debate about government growth. Foes of Washington bureaucrats preferred local government, feeling it more responsive to popular needs.

But local government is characteristically the government of the locally powerful. Historically, the locally powerless have often won their human and constitutional rights by appealing to the national government. The national government has defended racial justice against local bigotry, upheld the Bill of Rights against local vigilantism, and protected natural resources from local greed. It has civilized industry and secured the rights of labor organizations. Had the states' rights creed prevailed, perhaps slavery would still exist in the United States.

Americans are still of two minds. When pollsters ask large, spacious questions—Do you think government has become too involved in your lives? Do you think government should stop regulating business?—a sizable majority opposes big government. But when asked specific questions about the practical work of government—Do you favor Social Security? Unemployment compensation? Medicare? Health and safety standards in factories? Environmental protection?— a sizable majority approves of intervention.

We do not like bureaucracy, but we cannot live without it. We need its genius for organizing the intricate details of our daily lives. Without bureaucracy, modern society would collapse. It would be impossible to run any of the large public and private organizations we depend on without bureaucracy's division of labor and hierarchy of authority. The challenge is to keep these necessary structures of our civilization flexible, efficient, and capable of innovation.

More than 200 years after the drafting of the Constitution, Americans still rely on government but also mistrust it. These attitudes continue to serve us well. What we mistrust, we are more likely to monitor. And government needs our constant attention if it is to avoid inefficiency, incompetence, and arbitrariness. Without our informed participation, it cannot serve us individually or help us as a people to attain the lofty goals of the Founding Fathers.

CHAPTER 1

An Important Office

IN MARCH 1993, A TALL WOMAN placed her hand on a Bible held by her young niece and took a solemn oath of office in Washington, D.C. The woman's face, although smiling, was set firm with a sense of purpose and responsibility. She was being sworn in as America's new attorney general—the chief law enforcement officer of the United States government. She knew her task would bring challenges, tough decisions, and harsh criticism. But she believed she could do something for her country in this new role.

Seventy-five United States attorneys general had served before Janet Reno during the nation's first two centuries. But this swearing-in ceremony was remarkable. Reno was becoming the federal government's first female attorney general. It was an appropriate symbol of the change that has taken place over the years in this difficult post. U.S. laws have changed, and the legal concerns that face the country have shifted with the decades. At no time has the role of United States attorney general been more necessary . . . or more controversial.

One Part of a Powerful Cabinet

The U.S. attorney general is the head of the United States Department of Justice. As such, the attorney general is a member of the president's cabinet.

What is the presidential cabinet? You might think of it as the most powerful committee in the nation—probably in the world. This group consists of the U.S. government's 14 federal department heads, joined by the country's representative to the United Nations. Together, they meet regularly to keep the president informed of what's happening in their areas of government, to share their views and knowledge on important matters, and to advise the president in making important decisions.

The president selects, or nominates, individuals to serve in the cabinet. Cabinet nominees then must be approved by a two-thirds majority of the United States Senate before they can take office.

What Does the Attorney General Do?

In simple terms, the attorney general is "boss" to all of the country's United States attorneys, U.S. marshals, and other federal court officers.

The attorney general advises the president concerning legal matters. For example, the president wants the attorney general's opinion before appointing individuals to be federal judges. Federal judges are appointed by the president. Many of our presidents have relied on their attorneys general or deputy attorneys general to research and suggest candidates for federal judgeships.

This is a complicated task. Care must be taken that a nominee's record of rulings in court cases agrees with the

The Supreme Court in Washington, D.C., is our country's highest court of justice. Being the top lawyer in our government, the attorney general often becomes involved in trials which appear before the Supreme Court.

president's own views on key legal issues. At the same time, a nominee must be found who will be approved by the United States Senate. As in the case of cabinet appointees and other high government officials, a Senate majority must vote for approval before the person selected can become a judge.

The president also appoints United States attorneys for each federal district. These important officials work under the guidance of the attorney general. The attorney general appoints assistant U.S. attorneys to help them.

Other Kinds of Government Lawyers

Directly beneath the attorney general is the deputy attorney general. Third in rank is the U.S. solicitor general. The solicitor general and his or her assistants have a special function: they represent the government in cases before the U.S. Supreme Court. In especially important cases, the attorney general may appear personally before the Supreme Court on the government's behalf.

In England, the functions of the attorney general are handled by a barrister who only serves the queen. Here, a group of barristers prepare for ceremonies in England's House of Lords.

You may hear in the news of other people besides Janet Reno or her successors who are identified as "attorney general." Possibly, this person is your state's attorney general. Each American state has such an official. The state attorney general has a job very similar to that of the U.S. attorney general. At the state level, the attorney general must advise the state's governor on legal matters, bring lawsuits that have statewide significance, and function as the state's top legal officer.

There is a major difference, though, in how national and state attorneys general take office. While the U.S. attorney general is appointed by the president, 42 of our state attorneys general are elected by public vote. In the other eight states, they are appointed by their governors.

What About Other Countries?

America's attorneys general are not the only ones in the world. Most countries whose form of law is based on that of England have attorneys general. English kings were appointing them more than 500 years ago. In modern-day

Great Britain, the attorney general advises the queen or king and their royal ministers (government leaders) and represents the British royal government in court matters. The British attorney general is a lawyer, or *barrister,* and the queen (or king) is this lawyer's only client. So the British consider their attorney general to be the country's leading barrister.

This is similar to the way it works in America. But our system of government is notably different from England's. In order to understand better what the U.S. attorney general does, let's learn more about the attorney general's domain: the United States Department of Justice.

Saddam Hussein has complete control of Iraq and can make or remove laws in order to continue to hold power. The United States balances power with three separate branches of government, and the attorney general plays an important role in the judicial branch of our federal government.

CHAPTER 2

What Is the Department of Justice?

THE DEPARTMENT OF JUSTICE (DOJ) might be thought of as "America's law firm." Author Patricia C. Acheson, in her book on how the federal government operates, explains that the DOJ "can be compared to a very large law firm except for the fact that its clients are all the citizens of the nation."

Another author, Luther A. Huston, describes the DOJ's client base a bit more narrowly. The "single client" of the U.S. attorney general and staff, Huston writes, is "the government of the United States."

In either case, the DOJ clearly is a major law firm.

The American System of Justice

In America, we live under laws that are passed by our elected Congress. If "we the people" decide we don't like a particular law, we have the power (in theory, at least) to elect congressional representatives who pledge to change the law.

This is not the way laws are made in every country. Centuries ago in European kingdoms, a king could dictate a law (a "royal edict") all by himself. People in some countries today live under military governments and dictators— people who impose certain laws to keep themselves in power, not necessarily to serve the people's best interests.

In the United States, our law and government (called a *democracy*) are rooted in decisions made by elected officials. We believe we have the best, most people-oriented system of government in the world.

To ensure that our national laws are enforced fairly, we have the United States Justice Department. At the head of it is the U.S. attorney general. Within the department are such famous law enforcement bodies as the Federal Bureau of Investigation (FBI) and the U.S. Marshals Service.

Our First Attorneys General

You might suspect that we first invented a Department of Justice, then decided we needed a "general"—an "attorney general," since justice involves law—to run it. Actually, it happened the other way around. In 1789, Congress passed the Judiciary Act. Among other things, this important bill, or law, created the office of attorney general. Almost a century passed before there was a Department of Justice.

The U.S. Constitution never called for a presidential cabinet. It authorized the president to obtain written advice from his department heads: at that time, the secretaries of state, treasury, and war, plus the attorney general. Most of our first senators and congressional representatives believed the president would rely on them, not on the department heads, for advice.

George Washington, however, was more comfortable working differently. He preferred to discuss important questions in private with his department heads. By 1793, they had come to be known as Washington's cabinet.

The attorney general, our founders decreed, must be a "learned person, in the law." Our first attorneys general served mainly as the president and government's legal interpreters and advisers, not as our chief law enforcers. (Enforcement powers and agencies like the FBI came much later.) The attorney general also was required to prosecute government cases before the Supreme Court.

Although the Judiciary Act of 1789 did not say so, Congress believed the attorney general should give it, not just the president, legal advice. So for the first 25 years of United States history, our attorneys general were prominent figures in shaping national policies and in defining how our legal system would work.

But the early attorneys general did not receive special treatment. Their salary initially was $1,500 a year. That was a sizable figure for 1789—but out of it, the attorney general had to pay his office rent, clerk's salary, travel

Edmund Randolph, seen sitting to the far right, was our country's first attorney general and, as such, was a member of President George Washington's first cabinet.

expenses, and operating expenses. He had to buy the candles and lamps to light his office, coal for his fireplace, even paper and pens with which to write his opinions and other official documents. Not for 40 years was the attorney general given a special allowance to buy law books! He was expected to rely on his personal library for legal research.

Understaffed, the attorneys general gradually got behind in their work. In 1853, Attorney General Caleb Cushing frantically requested temporary clerks to help catch up on important record-keeping that had been accumulating for years. Congress eventually increased the office's clerical staff but was not happy about it.

Because of the low pay, our first attorneys general continued to practice law privately while in office, to maintain their incomes. In the early years, the attorney general was not required to live in the nation's capital. He was required only to be present when the U.S. Supreme Court was in session. This made it easy to continue in private practice. In effect, the office of attorney general was considered by many to be merely a part-time job.

William Pinckney of Maryland, U.S. attorney general from 1811 to 1814, took many cases to the Supreme Court during his law career—but always as a private counselor (lawyer), never on behalf of the government.

The Move Toward Forming a "Law Department"

As early as President Washington's time, many government leaders believed the new nation needed an official, national "law office" or "department of law." President Andrew Jackson in 1829 asked Congress to broaden the attorney general's powers greatly. Jackson wanted the attorney general to take charge of collecting money that was owed to the federal government. He also wanted the attorney general to supervise all criminal matters that involved the breaking of federal laws.

For the next 50 years, different presidents and cabinet officials pushed to expand the office of attorney general. It clearly was increasing in its importance to the government. In 1840, Attorney General Henry D. Gilpin collected into a book all the attorney general opinions that had been issued until that time. Thus, Congress and the public could refer to this volume of expert legal knowledge as a primary guide for answering law-related questions.

President James K. Polk proposed a national "law department" in 1845. But Congress, as before, refused. Our lawmakers feared that to expand the attorney general's duties and office would give that official too much power.

Finally, the Department of Justice was created by an act of Congress in 1870. President Ulysses S. Grant signed it into law. Amos T. Akerman became the first attorney general to serve as head of the DOJ.

Interestingly, Akerman and his successors until the end of the 19th century had to pay the office rent for the entire Department of Justice out of their own salaries. They worked in a building that sometimes went unheated during Washington, D.C.'s, bitter winter months.

Although since that time the attorney general has led a government department, her or his primary role has remained the same as always: serving as the federal government's chief lawyer.

Today's Department of Justice

The Department of Justice currently oversees six divisions:

The *Antitrust Division* makes sure American businesses operate fairly and don't attempt to get rid of or cripple their competitors. The **Antitrust** Division works closely with the Federal Trade Commission and other government offices on behalf of consumers (the buying public).

In 1870 the Department of Justice was officially created by an act of Congress. The Justice Department now finds most of its offices housed in the Department of Justice building in Washington, D.C.

The *Civil Division* deals with commercial and government agency problems as they relate to the federal government. It handles all lawsuits that involve the government. For example, if a federal employee is sued for wrongdoing while performing his or her duties, lawyers with the Civil Division defend the employee.

The *Criminal Division* is responsible for bringing to justice those who break federal criminal laws. Criminal offenses range from kidnapping to extortion (blackmail) to bank robbery. They include airplane hijacking; illegal trafficking (transport, sales, and distribution) in guns and certain drugs; racketeering (gangster activities); illegal gambling; saltwater fishing violations and other crimes on the "high seas"; and counterfeiting (illegally manufacturing money).

The *Civil Rights Division* must enforce laws that protect individual rights. It was created in the late 1950s, when African Americans were struggling to end racial **segregation.** The DOJ's **Civil Rights** Division focuses on legal issues that might threaten a person or group's equal rights based on their color, race, sex, national origin, or religion. Early civil rights cases dealt with the freedom of minorities to attend all public schools, use all public facilities, vote, obtain fair treatment in law courts, and obtain jobs. (Robert F. Kennedy, who we'll study later in this book, is the attorney general best remembered for his work to ensure civil rights.)

The *Environment and Natural Resources Division* enforces laws and policies in those areas. It often works with the Environmental Protection Agency (EPA) to make sure citizens and industries obey laws that were passed to protect our environment.

The *Tax Division* must see that our federal tax laws are obeyed. The Internal Revenue Service (IRS) ensures that every citizen is taxed fairly. When individuals or companies don't pay their fair share of taxes, Department of Justice lawyers can take them to court.

Each division is directed by an assistant attorney general. This assistant, like the U.S. attorney general, is appointed by the president. Each division has its own staff of lawyers and other employees who have special knowledge in their area of law.

Enforcing Justice

The DOJ has several law enforcement agencies:

The *Federal Bureau of Investigation* (FBI) is the best-known. Formed in the early 1900s, it first focused on wrongful business activities, and its agents were not authorized to carry guns. Soon, it was given power to investigate interstate crimes, gangster activities, kidnapping, and other violations. Today, almost 300 types of crimes are investigated by FBI agents.

The *Drug Enforcement Administration* (DEA), a newer agency, is increasingly in the news as it breaks up

narcotics rings. The DEA works with local and state law enforcement agencies as well as international police to prevent illegal drugs from entering the country and being distributed. DEA agents present public and school programs to educate citizens, especially young people, in the dangers of drug abuse and the violence caused by drug traffickers.

The *U.S. Marshals Service.* Our first president, George Washington, saw the need for official marshals to enforce laws in the new nation. Otherwise, law enforcement would be left largely in the hands of vigilantes, bands of armed citizens who took it upon themselves to chase down criminals. Some of our frontier crime fighters like Wyatt Earp were U.S. marshals with presidential appointments. Modern-day marshals must protect federal court officials, including judges, juries, lawyers, and witnesses. They must see that the courtroom and trial proceedings are secure, that jurors aren't affected by outside influences ("tampering"), and that criminal defendants do not escape and are not harmed. U.S. marshals also may be sent to areas of rioting or natural disasters to keep peace and order.

The **Immigration and Naturalization Service** (INS) makes sure foreigners enter America through legal channels and, if they intend to reside here, become official citizens. Those who don't meet requirements are "deported," or forced to leave the country. Related agencies under the DOJ include the *Board of Immigration Appeals* and the *Executive Office for Immigration Review.*

It's interesting that during its first century or so, the United States had no laws governing immigration. Congress became concerned about the large numbers of foreigners entering the country in the late 1800s. At that time, the nation's population was growing dramatically, and unsettled territory was vanishing. In large cities with many people living together at close quarters, health problems worsened as immigrants brought contagious diseases from Europe, Asia, and other parts of the world. Foreigners now are required to understand the American form of government and vow to abide by its laws before they can become U.S. citizens.

The DOJ also oversees the *Bureau of Prisons*, which administers our network of federal penitentiaries. And it operates the *Parole Commission*, a panel of nine of the president's representatives. The Parole Commission decides whether federal prisoners deserve to be released before they finish serving their sentences.

Helping the DOJ provide the best legal system possible is the *Office of Professional Responsibility*. This office looks into any charge that a federal judge, agent, lawyer, or anyone else in the Department of Justice may have done wrong. The idea is that if we are to have an excellent federal justice system, we must make sure our Justice Department consists only of people with unquestionable honesty and fairness.

Altogether, the attorney general supervises many thousands of lawyers, federal law enforcement agents, and support staff.

Is the System Fair?

You may be wondering: If federal courts and judges are part of the U.S. government, and the Department of Justice and its lawyers are also part of the U.S. government, how can a DOJ lawyer ever lose a case? Is a government judge likely to rule against the government's side of any argument?

Absolutely. Federal judges must ensure that justice is achieved for America's citizens. Persons and corporations who are opposed by government lawyers in federal courts enjoy the same legal rights as contestants in any other court. If they are defendants, they must be presumed

The Department of Justice recently took Microsoft and its CEO, Bill Gates, to federal court for practicing business which is unfair to its competitors. The Antitrust Division of the Justice Department oversees laws which keep corporations competitive and helps ensure fair business practices.

innocent unless the government's lawyers can prove them guilty beyond a reasonable doubt. If they are **plaintiffs** (people, companies, or organizations who accuse the government or its employees of wrongdoing), they have an opportunity to prove that the government is at fault.

Sometimes the government is wrong. Government officials and their lawyers are not perfect. Sometimes they base their actions on misinformation or bad judgment. When that happens, it is the duty of the federal court system to see that the wrongs are corrected.

A Significant National Leader

Naturally, attorneys general must possess excellent credentials as prosecutors or judges. Usually, they have talents and knowledge that qualify them for other high-level government posts as well.

No attorney general has ever become president, but 10 have been appointed to the U.S. Supreme Court—the highest court of law in the land. They were Roger B. Taney, Nathan Clifford, Edwin M. Stanton, Joseph McKenna, William H. Moody, James C. McReynolds, Harlan F. Stone, Frank Murphy, Robert H. Jackson, and Tom C. Clark. Taney and Stone served as chief justices of the Supreme Court.

Nine attorneys general were state governors: Edmund Randolph (Virginia), Levi Lincoln (Massachusetts), John J. Crittenden (Kentucky), Isaac Toucey (Connecticut), Augustus H. Garland (Kansas), Judson Harmon (Ohio), John W. Griggs (New Jersey), Frank Murphy (Michigan), and J. Howard McGrath (Rhode Island).

Interestingly, the attorney general is fairly high on the list of government officers who can succeed (replace) the president in times of emergency. If the president dies in office or becomes unable to carry out his or her duties, the vice president becomes president. If the vice president for any reason cannot take over as president or must be replaced, the Speaker of the U.S. House of Representatives (the highest-ranking House member) becomes president. If that person must be replaced, the president pro tempore of the U.S. Senate (the highest-ranking senator) becomes president.

In case none of those officials can perform as president, the "line of succession" next goes to the secretary of state, then the secretary of the treasury, then the secretary of defense, and then the attorney general, followed in turn by other cabinet officials.

It is extremely unlikely that any cabinet officer will ever become president in such an emergency. But the line of succession suggests the comparative importance of government officeholders.

John J. Crittenden served as attorney general for three different presidents. Appointed in 1841 by President William Harrison to his first term (which he served under Harrison successor John Tyler), Crittenden returned in 1850 as the attorney general for President Millard Fillmore.

CHAPTER 3

Meet Some of the Nation's "Top Lawyers"

LET'S TAKE A LOOK at some of the individuals who have served as U.S. attorney general. History remembers most of them as capable leaders in the pursuit of justice. Some are regarded as national heroes. Others left behind tarnished records.

Many attorneys general throughout history have found themselves in the thick of controversy. Sometimes it's because their decisions, though based on sound information, have led to unhappy results. Sometimes it's because their presidents' political enemies have found fault with the way they work. And sometimes it's because they simply made mistakes.

Edmund J. Randolph, Our First Attorney General

George Washington emerged from the American Revolution as a very popular army commander in chief and as the war's most outstanding hero. When Washington took office as our first president in 1789, he chose Edmund J. Randolph as the republic's first attorney general.

Randolph functioned mainly as an adviser whom Washington consulted on legal matters. There was no presidential cabinet at first. Soon after taking office, Washington asked Congress to establish a Department of State, Department of War, Department of the Treasury, and office of attorney general. Randolph and the heads of the other departments after several years became known as the president's "cabinet."

Like many of the country's founders, Randolph was worried that America might place too much power in the hands of one leader: the president. These skeptics feared that the new government, with its president, could turn out to closely resemble the English Parliament with its king. That was the system of government Americans had fought to escape. (They were uneasy, for instance, when newspapers referred to the president's wife as "Lady Washington.")

But Randolph agreed to support the new U.S. Constitution and to serve as the country's first attorney general. It was a period when the new president and Congress were feeling their way. The early government was quite different from what we have today.

Edmund Randolph advised President Washington to declare a policy of neutrality in world affairs. Washington, Randolph, and other leaders wanted to make sure the young nation stayed out of wars between the European powers. The United States had just fought a long, draining Revolutionary War. Victory in the Revolution left our nation weak, with little money or military power. Remaining neutral—taking no sides in other countries' fights—would avoid costly entanglements.

Randolph also helped persuade Washington to exercise his first veto power. In 1792 Congress was "reapportioning" itself—deciding how many representatives should come from each state, based on the population (number of people in each state). Randolph and Thomas Jefferson, Washington's secretary of state, believed Congress' plan for dividing up the representative posts was unequal. Washington asked these two men, along with Congressman James Madison, to compose a veto statement for him. Congress accepted Washington's veto and changed its apportionment plan.

Some historians consider Randolph a cool-headed peacemaker in the early cabinet. Washington's advisers—notably Jefferson and Secretary of the Treasury Alexander Hamilton—often were at odds. Randolph tried to understand both sides of important debates, and he refused to ally himself with any one cabinet member. Sometimes he would agree with Jefferson, sometimes with Hamilton. Although this prevented him from winning strong friendships (Jefferson called him a "chameleon"), Washington came to rely increasingly on Randolph's middle-of-the-road advice. He often asked Randolph to compose important proclamations.

After five years, Jefferson resigned from office and Randolph succeeded him as secretary of state. Soon, however, Randolph himself had to resign from service under pressure. He was accused of trying to sell national secrets to the French government—a charge that eventually was shown to be untrue.

Washington was devastated by the charge against Randolph, who had been almost like a son to him for many years. He accepted Randolph's resignation very sadly in August 1795. Randolph died in 1813.

Charles Lee, the Statesman's Defender

Born in Virginia and educated at what is now Princeton University, Charles Lee was the country's third attorney general. He served from 1795 to 1801 under our first two presidents, George Washington and John Adams. During that time the country was expanding, and the government was defining itself. Unlike Randolph, Lee was not convinced neutrality was the best policy for America. He believed the United States should stand up to other nations and go to war, if necessary, to protect American interests.

Lee had interesting careers before and after his term in the presidential cabinet. Before entering law practice and politics, Lee served as a naval officer during and after the American Revolution. He later was a government customs official, then a lawyer and state legislator. President Washington chose him to succeed William Bradford as attorney general.

The most interesting part of his record occurred several years after he left the cabinet. It was a time of stormy national politics, when congressional representatives and cabinet members clashed with the president—and with one another—over vital matters that would shape the new nation's future. One of the most controversial government figures was Aaron Burr of New Jersey.

Burr was an American soldier in the Revolution and later a lawyer. Elected to the U.S. Senate, he became a contender for president in 1800. As it turned out, he was elected vice president, while Thomas Jefferson became president.

During the 1790s, Burr had become a bitter enemy of Alexander Hamilton, another leading statesman. Burr killed Hamilton in a duel with pistols in 1804. He was charged with murder in New Jersey, where the duel had occurred. But he avoided prosecution and finished his term as vice president.

Soon, Burr was leading an expedition of men into the frontier. In 1806, he was accused of plotting to establish a new empire in the Southwest. This was considered by many to be an act of treason against the United States. President Jefferson—the man under whom Burr had served as vice president—ordered his arrest.

To defend him, Burr chose none other than Charles Lee, the former attorney general. The case was tried in 1807 before the chief justice of the Supreme Court. Burr

was quickly found innocent, but he lived the rest of his life in disgrace.

Aaron Burr, seen here fatally wounding Alexander Hamilton in a duel, later faced charges of treason and chose former Attorney General Charles Lee to defend him in court.

John J. Crittenden, the Man Who Served Twice

At this writing, America has had 42 presidents—and almost twice as many attorneys general. Because of controversies and disagreements, many cabinet officials have resigned or been fired before their presidents' terms expired. Some presidents have had three or four attorneys general during their administrations. Ulysses S. Grant had five!

With Attorney General John J. Crittenden, it was the other way around. He was called to serve as attorney general by two different presidents. In fact, he actually served under three.

Born in Kentucky not long after the American Revolution, Crittenden studied at the College of William and Mary in Virginia. He became attorney general for the

Illinois Territory (before Illinois became a state) in 1809. Later, he served in the Kentucky legislature, then the United States Senate.

Crittenden first was appointed United States attorney general by President William H. Harrison in 1841. Within weeks, Harrison died of pneumonia. Crittenden continued to serve under Harrison's successor, President John Tyler.

In 1850—two presidents later—Crittenden was asked to return to the post by President Millard Fillmore. This was the period when tensions were increasing between the North and the South, and America's leaders were trying to prevent a civil war. Among his other work, Crittenden is remembered as the author of the Crittenden Compromise, which sought to ease the problems without violence.

The efforts of Crittenden and others, of course, ultimately failed. A decade later, Americans went to war against each other. Crittenden spent his last years of public service as a member of the U.S. House of Representatives from 1861 to 1863.

Hugh Swinton Legaré: Overcoming Physical Adversity

Many American leaders have conquered physical challenges to make important contributions to the nation. Most notable, perhaps, was President Franklin D. Roosevelt, who guided the country through the crisis of World War II despite suffering from polio.

Hugh Swinton Legaré was an early example of a public servant who battled constant physical pain. As a five-year-old boy in Charleston, South Carolina, during the early 1800s, he was given a vaccination against smallpox, a dreaded disease. In those days, vaccinations and treatments sometimes were almost as dangerous as the illnesses they fought. An alarming reaction to the inoculation almost killed Legaré and left him permanently disabled.

Legaré did not grow very much for the next seven years of his life. As a teenager, he finally began to grow tall—but only from the waist up. After he reached manhood, a friend wrote, "his legs were so short that he seemed dwarfed." Legaré walked clumsily, and he was very self-conscious about his appearance. All his life he was in poor health, and he spent much of his time at health spas and "healing springs."

It did not prevent him from practicing law and participating in government and politics, though. He served for four years as a U.S. official in Belgium, then was elected to Congress. In 1841, President John Tyler appointed him attorney general.

Edward Bates: The Civil War Era

The most difficult and disastrous period in American history was the Civil War (1861–65). Abraham Lincoln, considered by many to be the nation's greatest president, served during the frightful war years.

Lincoln's election in 1860 prompted the Southern states to break away from the Union. Lincoln was an "abolitionist," a person who wanted to abolish (end) slavery. In the South, where thousands of slaves were used on large farms and plantations, abolitionists were unpopular. Southern leaders vowed that if Lincoln won the presidential election, they would "secede," or break away and form their own country, or a loose "confederacy" of states.

Although Lincoln expected the Southern states to secede, he hoped unity could be restored quickly, without bloodshed. He wanted Southerners to know he respected them and still considered them part of the United States. So, in selecting members of his cabinet, he looked for men from all parts of the country, including the "border states" located near the South.

Tall, white-bearded Edward Bates was a nationally respected statesman from Missouri, one of the border states. Bates was so popular, in fact, that he was one of Lincoln's leading challengers for the Republican presidential nomination in 1860. A former soldier, lawyer, Missouri state attorney general, and congressman, he was almost 60 years old during the heated presidential campaign that year.

Lincoln asked Bates to be his attorney general. He hoped this appointment would please the angry leaders of the South. He knew Bates had been born in Virginia, the leading Southern state. Now, as a Missouri statesman, Bates could also help Lincoln appeal to the West.

Bates was considered a moderate politician, eager to find ways for opposing sides to agree. He strongly criticized those who wanted to break ties with the Union, however, and he opposed slavery in new Western states and territories. His viewpoints were very much those of President Lincoln—unlike some members of the cabinet, who thought Lincoln was too forgiving toward the Southern rebels.

Bates believed the North did not need to fight at all in order to defeat the South. He thought that by blockading Southern ports to prevent goods from entering or leaving the Southern states, the Union could force the rebels to return to the fold. Bates and others who supported such a "painless" solution were disappointed when the nation became a battleground.

During the early years of the war, many of the legal issues confronting lawmakers and the attorney general involved slavery. Although most Northerners agreed slavery should be ended, they did not agree exactly how and when to do it. There were slave owners in the Northern states and especially in the border states. In fact, slavery still was legal in the nation's capital, the District of Columbia, during the first years of the Civil War.

Slave owners had paid a lot of money for their slaves, and they wanted to know who would repay them for their losses. There was disagreement about whether runaway slaves in the border states should be captured by federal law enforcement officers and returned to their owners. There were questions as to whether freed slaves were

The Civil War divided the country and turned the nation into a battlefield. Edward Bates served as attorney general during the course of the war and took on many of the legal problems that surrounded the issue of slavery.

United States citizens with the same rights as other Americans. Should former slaves who joined the Union army be paid the same as white soldiers and enjoy equal treatment? Americans, especially Northerners, did not agree on the answers to questions like these.

The arguments continued through most of the war years. In 1864, the year before the war ended, Bates resigned because of his age.

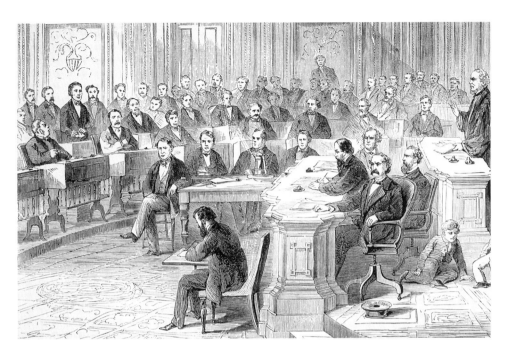

President Andrew Johnson chose his attorney general, Henry Stanbery, to defend him from impeachment before the Senate. Although the president avoided being removed from office, the Senate wouldn't allow Stanbery to return as attorney general.

Henry Stanbery: Defending the President

Often, government officeholders get caught up in politics. Political parties have differing views on how the country should be run. They constantly argue for their beliefs.

This adversarial political system (involving adversaries, or opponents) is healthy. It ensures that different viewpoints will be heard on major issues. It sometimes leads to anger and ill will among the politicians on opposing sides, however. Those in power try to hurt the political careers of their enemies, while those out of power try to embarrass officeholders.

After President Abraham Lincoln was assassinated in 1865, his vice president, Andrew Johnson, became president. Johnson was not very popular among members of the U.S. Congress. They disliked him so much, in fact, that they impeached him (tried to remove him from office).

Impeachment is a legal process. It is actually a trial of the president or other government official who is being challenged. Lawyers for Congress make their case against the president. Lawyers for the president then make their own case. Afterward, Congress votes on whether to remove the person from office.

Henry Stanbery was in the unhappy position of attorney general under President Johnson. Stanbery had been a lawyer for more than 40 years and state attorney general in Ohio before accepting the cabinet post under Johnson in 1866.

When Johnson was impeached, he asked Stanbery to be his chief lawyer. Stanbery resigned as attorney general in order to represent the president before Congress.

Johnson's presidency survived the impeachment proceedings. But the affair cost Stanbery his own job. Because he was the unpopular president's supporter, the U.S. Senate refused to approve Stanbery's reappointment to the cabinet position.

Alfonso Taft and the Troubled Election of 1876

You might know something of William Howard Taft, the 27th president of the United States. You may have heard little, though, about his father Alfonso, who also served his country at the national level.

Alfonso Taft was a prominent Republican judge and politician in Ohio during the 1870s. In 1875 he ran for governor but failed to receive his party's nomination. The following year, though, he was selected by President Ulysses S. Grant to be the nation's secretary of war.

Grant was completing his eighth year in the White House. Although he had been elected twice, Grant's administration would be remembered for a series of scandals. As secretary of war, Taft was replacing an army general who had been impeached for accepting a large bribe. After several months in office, Taft was asked to become attorney general—the fifth attorney general during Grant's stormy leadership.

Taft had a reputation for honesty. Grant hoped it would help improve the image of his tarnished presidency and that of the Republican Party. Grant and other Republicans were worried. In 1876, their major opponents, the Democrats, had for the first time since the Civil War a strong chance to win the presidential election. As it turned out, the election was one of the closest in history—and Alfonso Taft found himself in the middle of a frightening national crisis.

The Republican candidate was Rutherford B. Hayes, governor of Ohio and an old friend of Taft. The Democratic candidate, New York Governor Samuel J. Tilden, actually received some 200,000 votes more than Hayes. But the vote counts were disputed in three states. The winner in those states would be able to claim the election.

Both parties resorted to "dirty tricks"—bribery and bullying—in counting and recounting the votes. The arguments lasted for four months. Tensions ran very high. People feared the nation was headed for another civil war.

Congress finally agreed to name an electoral commission to decide the election. Taft, in his role as the nation's chief legal adviser at that moment in history, was involved in creating this important body.

The commission made an obviously "partisan" ruling (based on its political party ties). The Republicans prevailed. Hayes was named the winner.

Taft was criticized for his role in the election settlement, especially since Hayes was his friend. Many citizens thought (and many historians agree) that Taft and other Republican officials had "pulled some strings" through the election commission and, in effect, stolen the presidency from Tilden. Taft's son Will, the future president who was a college student at the time, himself questioned the "equity and justice" of the final outcome.

Although Hayes and Taft were political allies, Taft did not continue as attorney general. He was succeeded by Charles Devens, who served throughout Hayes' four-year term in office.

William Henry Moody, Prosecutor and Judge

Like Charles Lee, the attorney general who had defended Aaron Burr a century before, William Henry Moody was a noted lawyer in one of America's most famous trials. But while Lee worked for a noteworthy **defendant,** Moody was a prosecutor ("accuser") in a ghastly murder trial.

In the summer of 1892, the whole country was abuzz with news and rumors from Fall River, Massachusetts. Andrew Borden, a rich industry owner, had been murdered with an axe in his home. Also dead was his wife Abby. Charged with the horrible deed was 32-year-old Lizzie Borden, Andrew's daughter and Abby's stepdaughter.

The case caught the nation's interest for several reasons. First, naturally, was its stunning violence. Second, the Bordens were a wealthy, respected family, killed in their home on a sunny weekday morning for reasons that were unclear. Third, the accused wasn't just the victims' daughter—Lizzie Borden was a respected churchgoer with many friends who swore she wasn't capable of such an act.

Moody, who was district attorney for eastern Massachusetts, was one of two prosecutors assigned to the case. It was tried the following year. Remarkably, even though Moody lost the widely publicized trial—Lizzie Borden was found innocent—his career blossomed. Two years later he was elected to the United States House of Representatives. President Theodore Roosevelt selected him to be secretary of the navy in 1902; in 1904, Roosevelt made him attorney general. Two years after that, Moody became a member of the U.S. Supreme Court.

While Moody is remembered in popular history as the unsuccessful prosecutor in the Borden trial, he made notable contributions as a public servant. He pressed for U.S. naval bases to be created around the globe. As attorney general, he worked to break up industrial monopolies (companies or groups of companies controlling the market). And he was one of the most successful of our **trust-busting** attorneys general who began fighting illegal business and industry practices during the late 1800s.

Bonaparte, Stone, and the FBI

As we've seen, the U.S. Department of Justice has several law enforcement agencies. All of them function under the overall supervision of the U.S. attorney general. The best known is the Federal Bureau of Investigation (FBI).

The attorney general who officially started the FBI was Charles J. Bonaparte. He served under President Theodore Roosevelt early in the 20th century, first as secretary of the navy and later as attorney general, succeeding William H. Moody.

At the time, there was no national law enforcement agency to investigate federal crimes and apprehend violators. Almost all law enforcement in America was carried out by local and state police. What happened when someone broke a federal law outside the jurisdiction of any police force?

Bonaparte wanted to form a Bureau of Investigation, and in 1908, Roosevelt agreed it was needed. Made up of a few lawyers and former private detectives who had worked on government cases, the new bureau was a far cry from what it is today. Bonaparte was concerned at the time with antitrust violations (practices whereby big corporations used illegal means to snuff out their business rivals). His Bureau of Investigation looked into these business matters, as well as suspicions of lawbreaking inside the government by elected and appointed public officials. Bureau agents also were directed to investigate crimes that were committed on government property.

During the next 25 years, the bureau's powers and jurisdiction widened. The bureau began investigating suspected spies and individuals who organized attempts to overthrow the U.S. government. It played an increasing

The FBI is probably the most widely known agency of the Department of Justice. The FBI (although under another name) was created in 1908 when the attorney general at the time, Charles J. Bonaparte, recommended its creation in order to enforce antitrust laws.

role in catching "interstate" criminals, people and organizations who carried stolen and otherwise illegal goods from one state into another.

By 1924, the Bureau of Investigation had grown in importance and size. But the attorney general at that time, Harlan Fiske Stone, realized the bureau was not being run very effectively. He appointed J. Edgar Hoover to be the bureau director. Hoover, who served for almost half a century, is credited with building the FBI into a highly organized and efficient crime-fighting agency. The FBI is believed by many historians and journalists to be the best crime-fighting agency in the world.

During Prohibition, many of the nation's law enforcement agencies fought the illegal smuggling and creation of alcoholic beverages. Two different attorneys general served during this time and helped put gangsters and smugglers behind bars.

Sargent and Mitchell: Fighting Booze and Mobs

The U.S. Department of Justice, the attorney general's office, and the Bureau of Investigation (later called the Federal Bureau of Investigation) all grew and changed during the era of Prohibition.

Since the 1800s, many Americans had argued that the free use of alcohol caused drunkenness and countless related problems such as absences from work, violence and poverty at home, and worsening crime in the streets. In 1919, Congress passed the National Prohibition Act, banning the distribution and sale of beverages containing more than a tiny fraction of alcohol.

The result was a period of lawlessness across the country. Criminals realized they could make a lot of money by bringing liquor into the United States and selling it—illegally—to neighborhood bars and individuals. Unlawful booze in America became very big business.

Two of our attorneys general at the height of Prohibition were John Garibaldi Sargent and William DeWitt Mitchell. Sargent was appointed in 1925 by President Calvin Coolidge. Mitchell succeeded him in 1929 under President Herbert Hoover and served until 1933—the year Congress repealed (took back) the Prohibition Act.

During the Prohibition era, gangsters like Al Capone became powerful. In fighting them, "G-men" (government men) with the Bureau of Investigation and other federal agencies also became famous.

Legal Guidance Amid the World Wars: Gregory and Jackson

Twice during the 20th century, the United States was forced to take sides in world wars. Each time, the U.S. attorney general faced special challenges.

Thomas W. Gregory was named attorney general by President Woodrow Wilson in 1914 and served until 1919. An urgent concern during those years was national security. Many Americans were afraid of foreign spies and agents who might want to cripple the nation and prevent it from bringing its armed forces into the war. Gregory told Department of Justice investigators to be on the lookout for such people. An unusually high number of suspects were arrested as possible spies and "subversives" (people working to overthrow the government).

At the end of the war, Gregory was an adviser to U.S. officials at the peace conference in France. Their task was to decide on an agreement that would punish the nations that started the war and pave the way for world peace in the future.

World peace, unhappily, lasted only about 20 years. Germany, America's main opponent in World War I, rose to power quickly and began taking over neighboring countries. The result was World War II. Again, America and its allies defeated Germany and its allies after years of bloody fighting. This time, the world discovered afterward that German military leaders had committed horrible acts of violence against innocent civilians (nonmilitary citizens), not just in conquered nations but inside Germany itself.

Franklin D. Roosevelt was America's president before and during World War II. One of his attorneys general was Robert H. Jackson. Like Gregory, Jackson was from Pennsylvania. During the war, he served as attorney general, then was appointed to the United States Supreme Court. In 1945, when the war ended and Germany was defeated, the conquering nations began a series of trials of German leaders who had committed war crimes.

Jackson, because of his long experience as a federal lawyer and judge, was named chief prosecutor at the trials in Nuremberg, Germany. A number of brutal Nazis—members of the controlling German party during the war—were proven guilty of unspeakable acts. Some were imprisoned; others were executed. The work to find and prosecute German war criminals continued for many years.

Mitchell, Kleindienst, and Richardson: The Nixon Scandals

When Richard M. Nixon was elected president in 1968, he chose as his attorney general John N. Mitchell, a native of Michigan and one of Nixon's closest friends. He also had been the president's law partner in private practice.

Mitchell was a knowledgeable and capable attorney general. He is most remembered, however, for his disgrace in the political scandal known as Watergate. After burglars were caught breaking into Democratic Party campaign headquarters in 1972, they were linked to Nixon's cabinet.

Facing criticism and possible criminal charges for his part in campaign activities, Mitchell resigned as attorney general in 1972. In 1975, after being found guilty of criminal acts in the Watergate scandal, Mitchell was disbarred—forbidden to continue practicing law.

Nixon appointed Richard G. Kleindienst to succeed Mitchell in 1972. Kleindienst resigned the following year under pressure, also accused of misbehavior. He was convicted of giving false testimony during a Senate investigation and was sentenced to a short jail term, although the sentence was suspended (he did not actually have to go to jail).

Elliott L. Richardson succeeded Kleindienst at attorney general in 1973. He, too, left office quickly amid political turmoil. When Nixon ordered him to fire an official appointed to investigate the Watergate incident, Richardson refused and instead resigned from his post.

Nixon himself resigned the next year when it became obvious he would be impeached.

One of the most memorable attorneys general, Robert F. Kennedy took on issues from organized crime to civil rights during his short time in the position. He left a lasting mark on the attorney general's office but had his opportunity to continue his career tragically cut short.

CHAPTER 4

Robert F. Kennedy

JANET RENO MADE HISTORY at the end of the 20th century as America's first female attorney general. Probably the most famous attorney general of the century, however, served 30 years earlier.

Robert F. Kennedy immediately caught the public's interest for two reasons. First, he was President John F. Kennedy's brother. Second, both Kennedys were very young for their roles as national leaders. The new president was 43 years old; Robert, his choice for attorney general, was only 35. Some skeptics worried that they were too young for such enormous responsibilities. Within a year or two, though, few doubted them.

During his time as attorney general (1961–64), Robert Kennedy earned deep respect. He first became known as a fighter of organized crime. Later, he became a compassionate champion of civil rights. His career as a national public figure, which lasted less than eight years, carried him to the U.S. Senate and finally onto the campaign trail for president. But it ended abruptly and tragically.

A Young Government Lawyer

The seventh of nine children, Robert Kennedy was born in Brookline, Massachusetts, near Boston, in 1925. His family and friends—and later the American press and public—called him "Bobby." He earned his law degree at the University of Virginia Law School. In 1951, he became a lawyer for the Department of Justice.

During the next decade, Robert Kennedy emerged as a valuable DOJ prosecutor. He learned, from the inside, how government lawyers go about the task of ensuring justice for all the American people. During his years as a government attorney, he became a leading prosecutor in cases involving organized labor and management. Crime **syndicates** regarded him as an enemy. He also helped prosecute persons accused of "subversive" activities—efforts that threatened the American system of government.

Next Stop: The White House

His older brother John, at that time a United States senator from Massachusetts, decided to run for president in 1960. He asked Robert to be his campaign manager. Robert traveled from state to state during the primary elections, working long hours and leading the effort to put John F. Kennedy in the White House. The work paid off.

When John F. Kennedy was elected president, it seemed natural to him to turn to his brother Robert to serve as attorney general. Robert knew the work of the Department of Justice very well. He understood its challenges. He saw how the law was being trampled by power-hungry crime bosses, by people who hated other people because of their race, and by others who believed themselves to be above the law.

Attorney General Kennedy was aggressive in prosecuting the leaders of organized crime. Soon, though, more of his attention turned to civil rights problems. During this period African Americans were struggling—sometimes at the risk of personal injury—to win equal rights and treatment.

Battling Segregation

"Civil rights" refers to the rights and freedoms of a person or group of people within the main body of society. The word *civil* is related to *civilization*. American citizens—*all* American citizens—are guaranteed by our Constitution the right to say what they want and publish (in a newspaper, for example) what they believe. They may embrace whatever religion they wish. The Constitution also guarantees every American citizen the right to expect fair treatment in public—treatment no different from that enjoyed by anyone else. We all are equal in every way, under our form of government.

But until the 1950s and '60s, black citizens generally were granted less-than-equal rights. For example, they were allowed to ride only in certain seating areas (usually at the back) of public buses and trains. Many restaurants refused to serve them inside with white Americans; they had to go to a side door and wait outside if they wanted to buy a meal.

Many public school systems were segregated, or divided between whites and blacks. White students attended certain schools. Black students attended separate schools. In many situations, African-American schools were by no means equal to nearby all-white schools. Black schools might be given used desks and other furnishings—items discarded after the white schools had gotten the best use from them. Many teachers in black-only schools were not as well trained as teachers in white schools and were not paid as much for their work.

In 1962, police watch civil rights protestors kneeling to pray in peaceful protest against segregation in Albany, Georgia. While Robert F. Kennedy was attorney general, he fought to end the segregation of schools, colleges, and other public institutions.

Many colleges, especially in the South, admitted only white students. These usually were the most respected colleges—the ones with the most support money and therefore with the best equipment and the highest-paid and most knowledgeable professors. Young African Americans could attend segregated colleges, but their colleges would be less well-equipped and have fewer staff members. The result was that they could not expect an education equal to that of white students.

African-American leaders decided to break down the "color barrier" at all-white colleges. The U.S. Constitution guaranteed black students equality, so African-American leaders pressed for a system of integrated schools and colleges, where blacks and whites and people of all cultures and races could learn together, equally.

Thus, during the 1960s, more and more black high school students with excellent grades began applying for admission to all-white colleges. Some of the white college students and citizens, particularly in the South, did not like this change. In fact, some of them became angry and violent. There even were threats against the lives of black students.

As U.S. attorney general, Robert Kennedy was bound to protect all students as well as civil rights workers who were trying to help African American citizens vote freely in government elections. Several civil rights leaders were killed during this struggle. It was a period of terrible national stress and violence.

Throughout the troubles and uncertainty, Robert Kennedy was President Kennedy's closest adviser. He was a cabinet member and a trusted friend—and a blood brother who closely shared the president's dreams and concerns.

Sadly, it was a bond that would not last long. President Kennedy was shot to death in November 1963. The nation and the world grieved. In the minds of the public, Robert became the head of the large Kennedy family. Many people hoped he would continue his brother's policies as a national political leader. And so it happened.

A Leader in His Own Right

Robert Kennedy served for another year as attorney general under President Lyndon B. Johnson, who had been President Kennedy's vice president. Then he was elected to the U.S. Senate from New York. As a senator, Kennedy continued to work for civil rights. He also voiced strong opposition to America's growing involvement in the Vietnam War.

In Southeast Asia, Vietnam was a divided country. South Vietnam was an ally (friend) of the United States. North Vietnam was a Communist nation, opposed to the United States. North Vietnamese leaders wanted to take over South Vietnam and unite the country under its Communist form of government.

For years, the United States had sent army advisers to help South Vietnam defend itself from North Vietnamese forces. In the mid-1960s, the U.S. began sending soldiers to actually fight. More and more American military personnel were sent to Vietnam, and more and more were wounded and killed.

United States citizens at home were torn. Many, including President Johnson, believed we should defend South Vietnam in order to prevent Communism from spreading. Others believed it was a matter for the two small, far-away countries to settle between themselves, without American influence.

Sen. Kennedy sided with those who wanted to bring American soldiers home. He opposed Communism, but he believed it was an impossible situation for the United States.

The Final Campaign

In 1968, the senator decided to run for president. He promised, among other things, to end American involvement in Vietnam.

Kennedy's passionate pleas for peace and justice won him a growing number of followers during the Democratic Party's state-by-state primary campaigns. Early in June 1968 he won the most important state of all: California. He seemed certain to win his party's nomination.

He had only precious moments to celebrate, however. The night the primary voting returns were announced, Kennedy was approached by a man with a pistol in a

crowded Los Angeles, California, hotel. This man, an angry Jordanian who hated Kennedy's political message, was Sirhan Bishara Sirhan. Kennedy was shot in the neck. He died the next day. Sirhan was captured immediately. Tried and convicted, Sirhan at first was sentenced to death; the penalty was later reduced to life in prison.

Robert Kennedy died for the causes he believed in. He is remembered as an attorney general who was tough on lawbreakers and gentle toward the downtrodden. To many—especially those who have fought for civil rights— he is considered an American martyr.

Robert F. Kennedy Jr. touches the coffin of his slain father, Robert F. Kennedy. The senior Kennedy was assassinated in June 1968 and has been remembered by many as a hero in the pursuit of civil rights and peace.

CHAPTER **5**

Janet Reno

WOMEN HAVE SERVED IN cabinet posts since the time of President Franklin Roosevelt. But it wasn't until 1993, as we've seen, that a woman was appointed U.S. attorney general. President Bill Clinton first chose Zoe Baird as his attorney general nominee. When she withdrew during Senate questioning, Clinton picked Janet Reno. The Senate voted its approval unanimously.

From Family Crisis to Historic Moment

Reno had first been approached by Clinton's staff shortly after the November 1992 elections. Would she be interested in a role with the new administration? At the time, Reno was caring for her dying mother in Miami, Florida, while serving as state attorney for Dade County. She did not want to leave her home in this hour of family crisis.

Several months later, after her mother had passed away and the Baird nomination failed, the Clinton administration was still interested in Reno and her impressive record as a prosecutor. Reno commanded the respect of political liberals because of her efforts toward social improvement in southern Florida. She also earned the respect of political conservatives because of her strong crime-fighting record. She had a reputation for being a tough prosecutor—but also a fair one, sensitive to the problems of diverse people living in a sprawling, complex city like Miami. Long after her college years, she learned to speak Spanish because many citizens of the area were Latino. In fact, she sometimes delivered speeches in Spanish.

The president invited her to the White House. This time, she was ready to accept his nomination to the nation's highest legal post.

Spirit of Independence

Miami is Reno's hometown. The oldest of four children, she was born in 1938. Both her parents were journalists. They also were resourceful individuals who valued hard work and independence. Reno recalled how her mother, assisted by her father in the evenings when he returned from work, literally built the home they lived in near the Everglades. The cypress and stone house was built solidly to last—even through hurricanes. The house still stood after Hurricane Andrew's devastation in 1992. Reno proudly regards the house as her personal symbol that "you can do anything you really want to, if it's the right thing to do and you put your mind to it."

As a youth, Reno displayed qualities that make for excellent lawyering skills. As newspaper reporters, her parents loved family debates. Janet grew to become a high school debate champion and a college class leader. But she had several career interests. At Cornell University, she majored in chemistry, planning to become a doctor. By graduation, however, she had decided on a legal career. She entered Harvard Law School.

Early Work as a Lawyer

Law degree in hand, she went home to Florida. She began practice in a small firm and soon became a partner in the firm of Lewis and Reno.

In the early 1970s, Reno was appointed staff director of a committee of the Florida House of Representatives. Soon, she was trying her own hand at politics, campaigning for the state legislature. She lost that election, but she was not discouraged.

During the next few years, she served on a committee of the Florida State Senate. She also worked on the staff of a state attorney. Reno didn't realize it, but she was accumulating the kind of legal experience that would qualify her well for her later history-making role.

Reno became state attorney in 1978. Her Dade County office was the largest state attorney's office in Florida, processing more than 100,000 cases each year. The state attorney is responsible for prosecuting cases on behalf of the state government. Reno was in charge of about 90 lawyers when she took office. By the end of her 15 years there, she had a staff of more than 200 lawyers and about 900 other workers.

Busy State Attorney

Her work days were long. At night, she sometimes rode with police officers on patrol to observe law enforcement on the front lines.

While working to prosecute criminals, Reno realized there was much more to do in order to make life safer in Miami and the surrounding county. She spoke to school students and promoted programs to keep people—especially young people—clear of criminal influences. She also pressed for better living conditions and jobs for the poor, knowing poverty breeds crime. She worked hard to reduce violence inside homes. And she became very concerned about the growing problem of drug abuse.

Reno was so effective that she was reelected several times to the Dade County post. Her work came to the attention of Clinton campaign officials in 1992. Clinton described her as a "frontline crime fighter and caring public servant."

Reno as Attorney General

After she accepted Clinton's nomination, she quickly was approved by the U.S. Senate. She took office March 12, 1993.

Civil rights, environmental protection, children's protection, gun control, and the curbing of television violence have been some of Reno's main concerns as attorney general. Although she personally opposes the death penalty, she said before taking office that she would stand behind it in extreme cases.

Reno's approach to solving problems, she says, is "taking them apart and putting them back together again." She learned how to do that from her Harvard professors. Meanwhile, she is known by friends as a "down-to-earth" person. When she moved to Washington, D.C., she rented a one-bedroom apartment downtown and insisted on walking to work, regardless of the weather.

Dramatic Challenges

No attorney general has been without critical challenges. For Reno, probably the most serious one came within weeks after she took office.

Law enforcement officials from the FBI and the Bureau of Alcohol, Tobacco, and Firearms had surrounded the compound of a religious cult in Waco, Texas. Cult leaders had killed some federal officers and were believed to be heavily armed. The FBI asked the attorney general's permission to pump tear gas into the compound, hoping to drive out the cult members. After long hours of questions and discussions, Reno agreed.

Shortly after the tear gas was released into the compound, it exploded. Dozens of cult members, including 17 children, died.

Government and media investigations into what had happened lasted for years. Some believed the tear gas attack had set off the deadly explosion. Others said the cult leaders, willing to kill themselves and their followers for their radical cause, set fire to their own ammunition supply.

It was an extremely difficult situation for the attorney general. On one hand, federal law enforcement officers had been killed in the line of duty—and there had been fear of more deaths if the situation was not settled. On the other hand, some children had suffered violent deaths.

At this writing—seven years after the tragedy—the cause of the Waco explosion is still in question. Reno accepted full responsibility for the tragedy. She had given approval for the tear gas attack. Many citizens and congressional representatives criticized her. But many others believe she made the best decision she could at the time, and they respect her for accepting the blame. Whatever their opinion, no one could accuse Reno of dodging the issue.

The Branch Davidian compound in Waco, Texas, erupts into flames in 1993. Although the cause of the fire was unknown, Janet Reno accepted full responsibility for the tragedy, in which a number of federal agents and Branch Davidians perished.

Timothy McVeigh, seen here surrounded by law enforcement officials, was found guilty in 1997 for the bombing of the Alfred P. Murrah building in Oklahoma City, Oklahoma. Janet Reno and the Justice Department were praised for their swift apprehension and punishment of McVeigh following the bombing.

Continuing the Cause of Justice

Today the tradition of a forceful legal professional leading the nation's justice system continues. From Edmund Randolph to Janet Reno, United States attorneys general have had to make hard decisions based on the best information available. They've had to find the way for America's system of justice in the face of change. Each generation of Americans has introduced new legal questions. Our Department of Justice has to thread its way through an ever-changing maze of problems and challenges.

The attorney general, our legal pathfinder, must take the heat. For this lawyer/leader, there always will be frequent criticism and little public credit—at least, not in the official's lifetime. Only history can tell how effectively an attorney general has served. Until that record is written, the country's foremost law enforcement official must be content with a personal satisfaction that he or she performed ably and was faithful to our Constitution.

Glossary

Antitrust–The prevention of big businesses and industries from forming partnerships ("trusts") in order to unfairly drive out their competitors.

Civil rights–The rights of liberty for each citizen of the country. Among other laws, the 13th and 14th Amendments to the U.S. Constitution guarantee our civil rights.

Defendant–Person or organization accused in court of an unlawful act.

Immigration and naturalization–The process of moving into a country and becoming a citizen.

Narcotics–Strictly speaking, narcotics are drugs that dull the senses. They sometimes are prescribed by doctors but often are sold and used illegally. In law enforcement, the term "narcotics" usually refers to illegal drugs.

Plaintiff–Person, group, or organization who brings a legal complaint in court.

Prosecute–To bring a legal charge against an individual or organization and attempt to prove the charge in court. In typical criminal and government trials, the defense attorney represents the accused. The prosecuting attorney, or *prosecutor*, represents the accusing side.

Segregation–The policy of sending people of different races or sexes to separate schools and colleges, making them stay at separate hotels, and eat at separate restaurants, etc. Segregation practices were the major target of America's civil rights movement during the 1950s and '60s.

Syndicate–A network of organized criminals.

Trustbusters–Attorneys general and other government leaders who fought to break up illegal industrial monopolies, or "trusts," thus improving fair business practices.

Further Reading

Acheson, Patricia C. *Our Federal Government: How It Works*. New York: Dodd, Mead & Company, 1984.

Feinberg, Barbara Silberkick. *The Cabinet*. New York: Twenty-First Century Books, 1995.

Meachum, Virginia. *Janet Reno: United States Attorney General*. Springfield, NJ: Enslow Publishers, Inc., 1995.

Severn, Bill. *William Howard Taft: The President Who Became Chief Justice*. New York: David McKay Company, Inc., 1970.

Simon, Charnan. *Janet Reno: First Woman Attorney General*. Chicago: Children's Press, 1994.

ABOUT THE AUTHOR: Daniel E. Harmon is the author of 18 nonfiction books on topics ranging from history to humor. He also is the editor of *The Lawyer's PC*, a national technology newsletter, and associate editor/ art director of *Sandlapper: The Magazine of South Carolina*. Harmon lives in Spartanburg, SC.

SENIOR CONSULTING EDITOR Arthur M. Schlesinger, jr. is the leading American historian of our time. He won the Pulitzer Prize for his book *The Age of Jackson* (1945) and again for *A Thousand Days* (1965). This chronicle of the Kennedy Administration also won a National Book Award. Professor Schlesinger is the Albert Schweitzer Professor of the Humanities at the City University of New York, and he has been involved in several other Chelsea House projects, including the REVOLUTIONARY WAR LEADERS and COLONIAL LEADERS series.

Picture Credits